D1747594

Discovering Cultures

Australia

Sharon Gordon

BENCHMARK **B**OOKS

MARSHALL CAVENDISH
NEW YORK

With thanks to Frances Cushing, Research Associate, Edward A. Clark Center for Australian & New Zealand Studies, University of Texas, for the careful review of this manuscript.

Marshall Cavendish
99 White Plains Road
Tarrytown, New York 10591-9001
www.marshallcavendish.com

Text copyright © 2005 by Marshall Cavendish Corporation
Map and illustrations copyright © 2005 by Marshall Cavendish Corporation

All rights reserved. No part of this book may be reproduced or utilized in any form or by any means electronic or mechanical, including photocopying, recording, or by any information storage and retrieval system, without written permission from the copyright holders.

All Internet sites were available and accurate when sent to press.

Library of Congress Cataloging-in-Publication Data

Gordon, Sharon.
Australia / by Sharon Gordon.
p. cm. — (Discovering cultures)
Includes bibliographical references and index.
ISBN 0-7614-1791-5
1. Australia—Juvenile literature. I. Title. II. Series.
DU96.G67 2005
994—dc22   2004006136

Photo Research by Candlepants Incorporated
Cover Photo: L. Clarke/*Corbis*

The photographs in this book are used by permission and through the courtesy of; *Corbis*: Paul A. Souder, 1, 20 (both), 24, 25, 27, 43 (lower right), back cover; Paul Steele, 4, 36. L. Clarke, 6, 42 (center); David Bell, 7; John Carnemolla 8, 43 (left); Martin Harvey, 9, 11, 19; Penny Tweedy, 10, 14; Staffan Widstrand, 12; Robert Essel NYC, 13; Roger Garwood & Trish Ainslie, 15; Lightstorm/Australian picture Library, 16; David Samuel Robbins, 18; Christine Osborne, 21; Patrick Ward, 26; Sean Davey Australian Picture Library, 29; Arko Datta/ Reuters, 30; Sergio Pitamitz, 32; John Van Hasselt, 33; Ralph A. Clevenger, 37. *The Image Works*: Kyoko Haga/HAGA, 17; Hideo Haga/HAGA, 34, 35, 39; Mike Leonard/HAGA, 38. *Brooks Walker/Envision*: 22.

Cover: *Opera House, Sydney, Australia*; Title page: *Australian schoolboy*

Map and illustrations by Ian Warpole
Book design by Virginia Pope

Printed in China
1 3 5 6 4 2

Turn the Pages...

Where in the World Is Australia?	4
What Makes Australia Australian?	10
Living in Australia	18
School Days	24
Just for Fun	28
Let's Celebrate!	34
The Flag and Money	40
Glossary	41
Fast Facts	42
Proud to Be Australian	44
Find Out More	46
Index	47

Where in the World Is Australia?

Australia is the smallest of the world's seven *continents*. It is also the largest island in the world. It is about the size of the United States, without Hawaii and Alaska. Australia is in the southern hemisphere between the South Pacific and Indian Oceans. Its seasons are the opposite of those in the U.S., with summer in December and winter in July. Australia's nearest neighbors are Papua New Guinea, Indonesia, and New Zealand.

Australia's climate changes from place to place, but it is generally warm and dry. Much of the land is desert, or semidesert. These areas are called the outback. The weather on the eastern and western coasts does not get too hot or too cold. Large forests of low trees grow. Australians call these areas

Darling Harbour in Sydney, Australia

Map of Australia

the bush. Since so much of the land is hot and dry, there are not many people living in Australia. Although it is close in size to the United States, Australia has less than one-tenth of its people. Most Australians live near the coast, where the oceans bring cooler, wetter weather.

Australia is the flattest continent in the world. It has only one major mountain range, the Great Dividing Range. These mountains run from north to south along the eastern side of the country. In the north, the land is made up of large hills and *plateaus*. But as they move south, the hills turn into rugged valleys and steep ridges called the Australian Alps. Australia's tallest peak, Mount Kosciusko, is in the Australian Alps. It is 7,316 feet (2,231 meters) tall.

The Great Western Plateau covers two-thirds of Australia. It is a high, flat land made up of three major deserts: the Great Sandy, Great Victoria, and Gibson. This area receives less than six inches of rain each year. Most of the land is covered with a dry, red soil, but some grasses and shrubs grow.

In the desert

The Great Barrier Reef

    The Central Lowlands stretch from the Gulf of Carpentaria in northern Australia to the Murray-Darling Plains in the south. This area is also very hot and dry. Crops cannot grow. But deep under the ground is the Great Artesian Basin. Farmers are able to pump water from these natural wells with windmills. They get enough water to grow tough grass and shrubs for sheep to eat.

    The eastern coast of Australia is called the Eastern Highlands. The best farmlands in the country are in the highlands. Sheep and cattle graze on the large, grassy plains and wheat is grown. Australia's largest cities are on the east coast including Brisbane, Sydney, and Melbourne. The capital city, Canberra, is also in the east. Even though most of Australia is very dry, there are tropical rain forests in the north and the southeast. These areas might get up to 78 inches (198 centimeters) of rain per year.

    In the ocean along the northeast coast of Australia lies the Great Barrier Reef. It is the largest coral reef in the world, with more than 400 kinds of

Uluru, the largest rock in the world

bright and beautiful coral. It stretches over 1,200 miles (1,931 kilometers) in the Coral Sea.

Australia has many unusual rock formations. Right in the center of the continent is Uluru, which used to be called Ayers Rock. It is the largest rock in the world. It is 1.5 miles (2.4 km) long, 1 mile (1.6 km) wide, and about 1,142 feet (348 m) high. Uluru looks like it is glowing a deep red color. Visitors enjoy trying to hike up the rock, but many give up before they get to the top. To the Aborigines, Australia's first people, Uluru rock is a sacred place. They ask visitors not to climb on it.

Australia does not have many large lakes, since the climate is so dry. Lake Eyre is Australia's largest lake, but it rarely has any water in it. Most of the time it is a dry lake bed. Once every fifty years or so, heavy rains cause floods that fill the lake. When that happens, plant and animal life returns.

The Kookaburra

The kookaburra lives in the woods of eastern Australia. This gray-brown bird nests in the treetops and is known for its strange, laughing call. The kookaburra is called the bushman's clock because it sings a loud, eerie song at the same times each day. It sings each night when it returns to its nest and again at dawn. The Aborigines believe the bird's unusual call was meant to wake people up in time to see the beautiful sunrise. Besides their strange singing, kookaburras are popular for another reason: they like to eat snakes and lizards.

What Makes Australia Australian?

Australia is a country like no other. Its unusual weather, people, and animals make Australia *unique*. Its plants, animals, and people have had to adapt, or change, in order to live in such a hot, dry place.

A eucalyptus tree

Australia's famous kangaroo

    Some Australian plants have special ways of staying alive in so much sun with so little water. The bottle tree has a thick, round trunk where it stores water. Farmers know they can cut up the trunk to get water for their cattle during very dry periods. The *eucalyptus* tree is one of Australia's most famous plants. It is also called the gum tree. There are about 450 different kinds of eucalyptus. Each has adapted to its own environment. Eucalyptus trees have thick evergreen leaves that turn sideways to avoid drying out when the sun gets too bright.

    Since Australia is not connected to any other continent, many animals are only found there. The kangaroo is probably Australia's most famous animal. These amazing animals can stand 6 to 7 feet (1.8 to 2.1 m) tall and can jump up to 20 feet

(6.1 m) in one hop! Female kangaroos have large pockets in the front to carry their babies, called joeys. Animals that carry their young like this are called *marsupials*. Kangaroos can be seen everywhere, from the outback to the golf course. Instead of a road sign that says "Deer crossing," Australian drivers might see a warning for "Kangaroo crossing." The Australian airline, Quantas, has a picture of a flying kangaroo on its airplanes. The kangaroo is even on Australian money.

Another well-loved *symbol* of Australia is the soft and gentle koala. Since they look like cuddly teddy bears, many people call them koala bears by mistake. They are not bears, but marsupials, like the kangaroo. They are *nocturnal* and live in trees. The name *koala* means "one who does not drink." Koalas get all their food and water from the leaves of the eucalyptus tree.

A cuddly koala

Australia has other unusual animals. The emu is the world's second-largest bird. It stands about five to six feet (1.5 to 1.8 m) tall. The female emu lays the eggs, but the male emu hatches them. The Australian island of Tasmania, off the southeast coast, is known for its Tasmanian Devil. This marsupial is about the size of a small dog.

Australia is a new country. Explorers knew about the land in the 1500s. However, Great Britain did not claim it until 1770. Australia's first settlers were prisoners who were sent from England in 1788. Australia became a nation in 1901. Most Australians are descendants of the British.

When the British came, many Aborigines were forced to give up their land and culture. Today, Aborigines make up only 2 percent of the total population. But in

Aborigines using a laptop computer

The parliament building in Canberra

recent years, they have become an important part of Australian culture. Their art is displayed in museums. Their old languages are being taught once again. They have also gotten back some of the lands that once belonged to their tribes.

The Aborigines created one of Australia's famous inventions, the boomerang. This wooden club is shaped like a V and was mainly used for hunting. It could be thrown a long way. Pictures of animals or other symbols were often painted on the

People from many countries live in Australia.

boomerang. When it is thrown, its unique wing shape makes the boomerang come back to the thrower.

Australia's official name is the Commonwealth of Australia. It has a democratic government. The chief of state is Queen Elizabeth II, the ruler of Great Britain. The governor general represents the queen in Australia. The head of Australia's government is the prime minister. A parliament makes laws for the country.

Since World War II, Australia has become a more diverse nation. People from Italy, Greece, and other places have come to live in Australia. Some have come from Asia and the Middle East. This has brought changes to the Australian culture. There are new languages, religions, and types of food.

Australians are a friendly, outgoing people. They often call each other "mate," or friend. In the past, Australians used the word *mate* to remind them to help each other in difficult times. Today, the word *mate* is used to show friendship.

Good day, mate!

English is the official language of Australia. Australians have their own unique accent, just as Americans do. However, it does not change from one part of the country to another, like it does in the United States. They also use different words than other English-speaking nations and often shorten words. The mailman is called the "postie" and *arvo* means afternoon. A *billy* is a tin can that can be used to make tea at a picnic. Sometimes, visitors need help in understanding Australian words.

Dreamtime Magic

The Aborigines of Australia believe the world was created by spirits who now live in trees and rocks. They believe that by going into "Dreamtime," a person can talk with these spirits. Afterward, they tell others what they learned from the spirits through music, dance, and art. A corroboree is a celebration of Dreamtime. The Aborigines paint special designs on their bodies and dance to the music of the *didgeridoo*, a long hollow pipe made from a tree log. They beat clap sticks to keep the rhythm. They celebrate with a great feast.

Living in Australia

Australians living in the outback have very different lifestyles than those living in cities. They are far from any neighbors. A trip to the nearest town for shopping might only happen once a week. When they travel by car, they must be prepared with extra gas, food, water, and tools in case they break down. Like ranchers in the United States, they often use four-wheel drive cars that can travel over rough roads.

People in the outback use two-way radios to warn each other about wildfires or dangerous storms. They also use them to contact doctors when someone is sick. Each

A flooded road in the outback

region of the outback has a local outpost with a landing strip. An outpost may be a homestead, mining camp, or small hospital. If someone gets very sick or is injured, the Royal Flying Doctor Service (RFDS) sends a plane to the nearest outpost to help them.

Dingoes

People who live in the outback generally work in mines or on sheep or cattle stations. Australians call ranches "stations." Australia's 140 million sheep produce more than 70 percent of the world's wool. Male workers on a ranch are called jackeroos. Women are called jillaroos. Some stations have thousands of acres and large homes with rooms for visitors, studying, and storing food.

Australia has the world's largest fence. The dingo fence is 3,700 miles (5,953 km) long and runs from the southeast corner of Australia to Queensland. It was built to keep wild, yellowish dogs called dingoes from getting into southern sheep stations. The dingoes hunt and kill the sheep. Unfortunately, the dingoes have figured out how to dig under and through the fence.

Mining is one of Australia's major industries. Almost all of the opal stones in the world are mined in the outback of Australia. Coober Pedy in southern Australia is known as the opal capital of the world. It has people from more than forty nations living there. Diamonds and gold are also mined in western Australia. Half of all the world's sapphires come from Australia.

Many of the people who work in Coober Pedy live in underground homes or "dugouts." But they are far from simple caves! They have all

Left: A giant Australian opal

An opal mine in Coober Pedy

the things that regular homes have, such as electricity, full kitchens, carpets, and comfortable seating. The underground homes stay cool in the desert heat and save the owners a lot of money on air-conditioning.

Most Australians live in cities or towns. City living in Australia is not very different than living in the United States. People live in houses or apartments with their families. The living room is called the lounge. It is used for family activities, such as watching television or doing homework.

Before the arrival of citizens from around the world, most Australian meals were similar to those in England, with meat, potatoes, and vegetables. Today, Australians eat a variety of foods. Many people eat a lot of lamb, since there are so many sheep stations. They also enjoy going out to dinner. They can choose restaurants from many different cultures, such as Chinese, Greek, French, or Italian.

Houses and apartment buildings in Sydney

Pavlova, a summer dessert

    Australians begin their day with breakfast, or "brekkie." But most Australians would have a "cuppa" tea, juice, cereal, or toast with Vegemite. Vegemite is a favorite vegetable spread. On stations or farms, they might have eggs and some kind of meat, like snags (sausages) or bacon. For lunch, they might have a sandwich, a bowl of soup, or a plate of fish and chips. Children enjoy snacks like Popsicles, called icy poles, or some "lollies," which are candy and sweets.

    Take-away shops are very popular in Australia. They sell traditional food, such as meat pies with tomato sauce, or ketchup. Corner stores called milk bars are also very popular in Australian cities. They sell food and household goods. Australians also go to large supermarkets like those in the United States.

Let's Eat!
Pavlova

Pavlova is a dessert invented in Australia. It is named after the great Russian ballet dancer Anna Pavlova. Pavlova is a summer holiday dessert—it appears on many dinner tables during Christmas.

3 egg whites
1 pinch salt
3/4 cup castor (superfine) sugar
1/4 cup white sugar
1 tablespoon corn flour
1 teaspoon lemon juice
1/2 pint cream
kiwifruit or strawberries

Preheat the oven to 300 degrees Fahrenheit (the temperature is reduced for baking). Beat the egg whites until foamy. Add the salt and beat until soft peaks form. Slowly beat in the castor sugar, beating well after each addition. Keep beating until the mixture is stiff and the peaks stand up when the beater is removed. Mix together the white sugar and corn flour. Lightly fold into the meringue with the lemon juice.

Line an oven tray with baking paper. Spread the meringue into a circle and pipe a decoration around the edge or swirl with a spoon if desired. Bake in a cool oven (180 degrees Fahrenheit) for two to two and a half hours. Turn off the heat and leave in the oven overnight to cool.

Top with whipped cream and decorate with sliced kiwifruit, sliced strawberries, passion fruit, or just about any tropical fruit, just before serving.

School Days

Children in Australia receive an excellent education. Ninety-nine percent of the children can read and write. Most Australians go to public schools, which are free. About one-third go to independent or private schools. These may be run by the Roman Catholic Church or other religions. Many schools have uniforms, and those that do not, have a dress code.

Australian children must go to school between the ages of six and fifteen. They go to primary school for six years. Then they go to secondary school for another five or six years. Primary schoolchildren usually start the day at 9:00 A.M. with an assembly for the whole school. After assembly, they go to their own classrooms. They have a short recess in the morning called play lunch. They continue with classes until lunchtime, and finish the day at 3:30 P.M.

After primary school, children attend a secondary school or a technical school. They do not have to complete secondary school, and some students leave before

Students in Melbourne take a lunch break.

finishing. Students in secondary schools study the same subjects as do students in the U.S. These subjects may include English, math, science, geography, history, computer science, or language. Some schools have begun to include classes on Aboriginal history and culture.

Children who live close by walk to school. Others are driven in cars. Children who live in suburbs or rural areas may take the bus to school. The idea of a "Walking School Bus" is being encouraged in some areas of Australia. Children walk to school in groups, along with parent volunteers. The parents are trained in safety and wear brightly colored uniforms. Australians hope the "Walking School Bus" will help solve traffic jams and provide more exercise for children.

After school, many children are involved in other activities. Some take music or acting lessons. Many sports are held after school. Australian schoolchildren can pick from sports like rugby, soccer, netball, basketball, field hockey, baseball, cricket, golf, and swimming. Minkey-hockey is also popular. It is like field hockey, but with easier rules for boys and girls to play when they are young.

Waiting for the train

A student speaks to her teacher on a two-way radio.

Some children live so far out in the outback they cannot go to a regular primary school, so they tune in to Australia's "School of the Air." They use two-way radios to talk to their teachers and classmates. They ask and answer questions for about an hour and a half each day. There might be a dozen children listening at once. They are given homework from their workbooks to do after the lesson. When school is over, these children usually help out on their farms and stations. As they get older and are ready for secondary school, they might go to boarding schools in the nearest town and come home on the weekends.

Australian children get their biggest school break from Christmas to early February. Since Christmas and New Year's are in the summer, many families are off from school and work. They take long vacations then and travel.

About 30 percent of Australians go to university, or college, after finishing secondary school. Some students go on to learn a technical skill or trade. Australia has more than thirty colleges and universities. Two of the oldest are the University of Sydney and the University of Melbourne.

Sing Like a Bird

This song is a favorite of young schoolchildren. The "gumdrops" that the kookaburra eats in the song are beads of sap that form on the eucalyptus, or gum, tree.

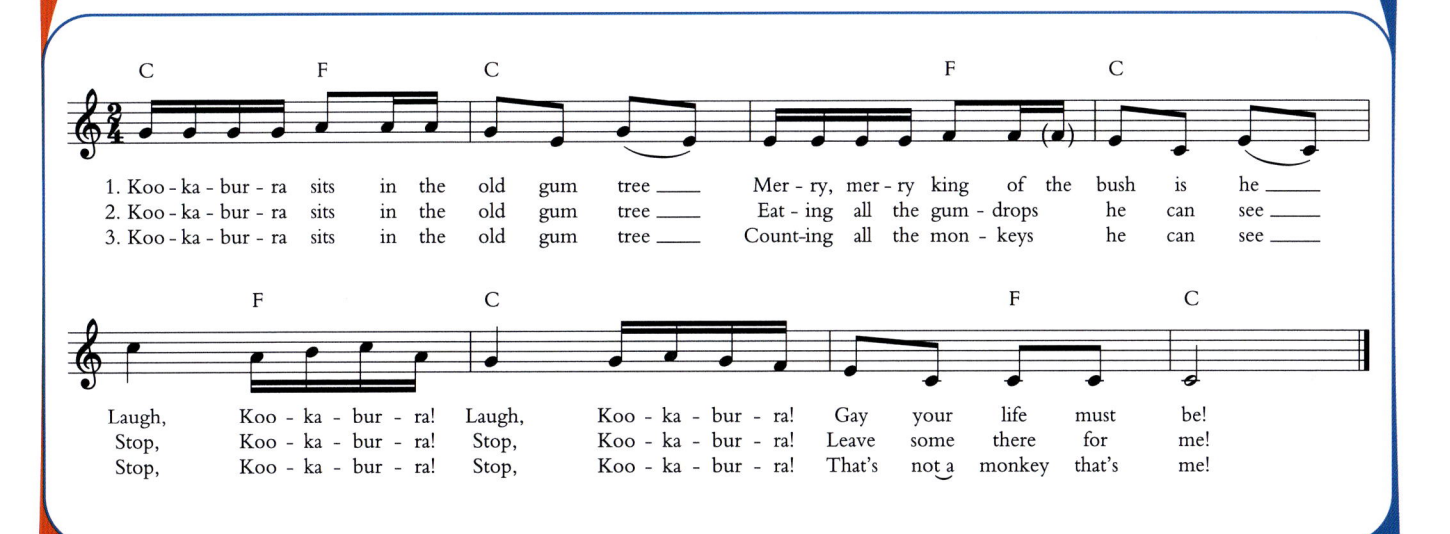

1. Koo - ka - bur - ra sits in the old gum tree ___ Mer - ry, mer - ry king of the bush is he ___
2. Koo - ka - bur - ra sits in the old gum tree ___ Eat - ing all the gum - drops he can see ___
3. Koo - ka - bur - ra sits in the old gum tree ___ Count - ing all the mon - keys he can see ___

Laugh, Koo - ka - bur - ra! Laugh, Koo - ka - bur - ra! Gay your life must be!
Stop, Koo - ka - bur - ra! Stop, Koo - ka - bur - ra! Leave some there for me!
Stop, Koo - ka - bur - ra! Stop, Koo - ka - bur - ra! That's not a monkey that's me!

Just for Fun

In a land with so much coastline, it is no wonder that going to the beach is a popular pastime. Swimming, surfing, *snorkeling*, scuba diving, and boating are how many Australians spend their holidays and free time. Lying in the sun is called

Bondi Beach

Catching a wave

sunbaking instead of sunbathing. Australia has a very high rate of skin cancer, so people do not sunbake as often as they did in the past. They also protect themselves by wearing suntan lotion. Bondi Beach is one of the most well-known spots for surfing and swimming. Surfing is very popular with teenagers and young adults. The warm coastal waters may have sharks, so huge underwater nets are set up to protect swimmers at crowded beaches.

Australians are known for their love of barbecues, or "barbies." They enjoy being outdoors in the warm climate and grilling with friends. Most homes have their own backyard grill for cooking. Australians barbecue on the beach and at parks. Some restaurants even let customers barbecue their own meat. Most large cities are close to the coast, so fish is popular to barbecue. Cattle and sheep farms give Aussies a great supply of beef and lamb. "Chook," or chicken, is popular, too.

Sports are a big part of life in Australia. People of all ages play sports. The game of cricket came to Australia with the British. It is played in the summer, from October to March. The game is played with a bat, a ball, and two wooden wickets. They are guarded by the batsman who tries to stop the ball from hitting the wicket. The top Australian prize in cricket is called the Sheffield Shield.

Tennis is also a very popular sport in Australia. The Australian Open is held each January in Melbourne. It brings crowds from all over the world. It is one of the four events in the Grand Slam Tournaments. To be a Grand Slam winner, a player must win the U.S. Open, Wimbledon, the French Open, and the Australian Open.

People who live in the outback must make their own fun. They are too

A cricket player takes a shot.

Cooling off in a local swimming hole

far from a town or their neighbors to be able to sit and chat. Their homes often have swimming holes or swimming pools for cooling off. They may have lots of board games and books. Many outback homes have a satellite dish, so they may get more channels than people in the cities. Fishing, hunting, and horseback riding are very popular. On special occasions, a few local families might get together for a barbie where the children get a chance to play with neighbors.

    City dwellers spend their weekends and holidays in much the same way as Americans. They play sports or watch them on television. They visit friends and relatives. They go to the beach to swim and surf. They go to museums, restaurants,

Sydney Opera House and Harbour Bridge

zoos, the ballet or symphony, the theater, or a rock concert. Even though Australia's mountains are not very high, they are still good for skiing in the winter. For some, Sunday is a day to go to church and have a family dinner.

The Sydney Opera House is a famous Australian landmark. It sits in Sydney Harbour near the Harbour Bridge. This unusual building took fourteen years to build and was finished in 1973. The building design looks like the sails of a ship sitting in the harbor. It is one of the busiest theaters in the world, with plays, operas, musicals, and ballets. It is one of Australia's main tourist attractions.

Australian Rules Football

Australians love football so much they made up their own form of it. "Aussie Rules" or "footy" is a main winter sport. It is an exciting, fast-moving sport that is a mixture of soccer, rugby, and basketball. It was invented in 1858 and is the major sport in many Australian states. Its popularity is spreading to Great Britain and the United States. There are eighteen players per team, with thirty-six on the oval field at once. Aussies follow their favorite football games and teams on the radio and television. Children cheer for their favorite players and wear their teams' jerseys.

Let's Celebrate!

Christmas takes place in the Australian summer, so Christmas shopping is done in T-shirts and shorts. Stores are decorated with snowmen and reindeer. Some families may spend Christmas Day outdoors enjoying the blue skies and sunshine. Others may go to the beach to swim and surf. Christmas dinner may be a barbecue or the traditional meal of turkey and plum pudding. Some have a picnic on the beach with salads, seafood, or cold meat. In Sydney, it is a tradition for people to go to the popular Bondi Beach on December 25.

Australian Christmas cards and pictures may show Santa Claus wearing a bathing suit or riding a surfboard. Instead of coming down the chimney, Santa comes in through the front door. Children leave him cookies and milk

A Christmas tree in summer

Sail away, Santa!

for his journey. He leaves them presents in their stockings or under the Christmas tree, which may be just an arrangement of fresh pine branches. Families sing Christmas carols. One popular song tells how Santa's sleigh is pulled by white *boomers*, or kangaroos, instead of reindeer.

The summer weather lets Australians use beautiful, fresh flowers to decorate their homes for the holidays. In some areas, the jacaranda blossoms are in full bloom in December. Australians also like to display the Christmas Bush, a native plant that has small, red leaves. Children search for the brightly colored Christmas beetles that eat the leaves of eucalyptus trees.

Fireworks over Sydney

The day after Christmas is called Boxing Day. The name comes from the English tradition of rich families putting their leftover food in a box for the poor. These days, Australians may give tips or a gift to their mailman or to the person delivering the newspaper. Many department stores also hold "Boxing Day" sales.

Australia Day on January 26 is Australia's most important holiday. It remembers the settlement of Australia in 1788 when Captain Arthur Phillip landed at Sydney

Cove with a large group of men and women. Australia Day celebrates what makes the nation great: its history, its people, and its spirit. It is a community day with flag-raising ceremonies and awards. There are many local events and activities. Australians who gather in Sydney Harbour enjoy fireworks and sing the national anthem.

On April 25, Australians celebrate ANZAC Day. ANZAC stands for the Australian and New Zealand Army Corps. Originally ANZAC Day was to honor the soldiers from

Veterans march in an ANZAC Day parade.

Horse racing at Melbourne

both countries who died in World War I. Now soldiers who fought during any war are remembered. Veterans march in parades through the streets.

Melbourne Cup day is also a holiday in Australia. This famous horse race brings hundreds of racing fans to Melbourne. Some people have picnics to celebrate and watch the race on television.

Each of the Australian states holds a yearly agricultural show, like the state fairs in the United States. There are prizes for the best cows, the largest bulls, or the sheep with the best fleece. Often, there is a log chop, which is a race to see who can cut a log in half the quickest. Sheep *shearing* contests are also held.

Carols by Candlelight

"Carols by Candlelight" is an Australian tradition. It started in 1937 when Norman Banks, a radio announcer, saw a lonely old woman listening to Christmas carols on the radio while a single candle burned in her window. It has become an annual event enjoyed all across the nation. Thousands gather in Sydney on Christmas Eve to sing carols and hold candles. On the last song, they hold hands, wave their candles, and sing "Let There Be Peace on Earth and Let It Begin with Me." The event is broadcast on television and radio. It is a wonderful display of love and national spirit. It is used as a fund-raiser for many charities.

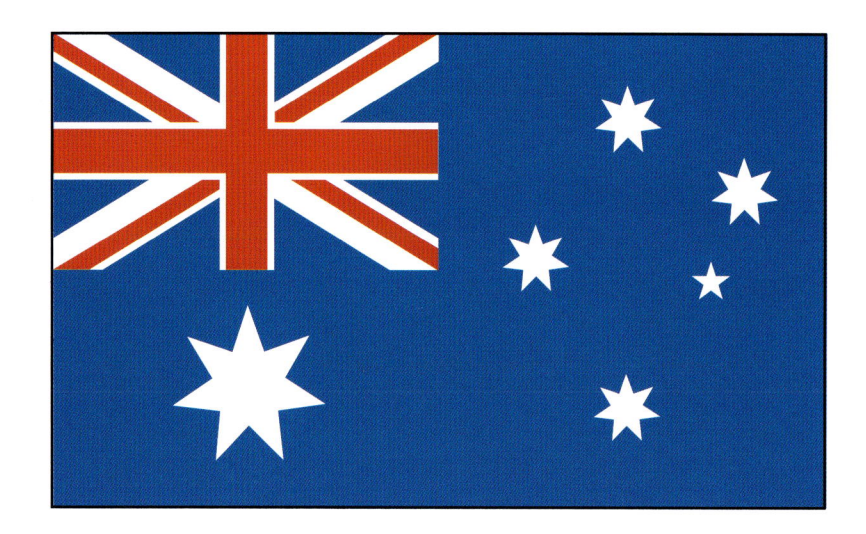

In the top left corner of the flag is the Union Jack, the British flag. It shows Australia's link to Britain. The right half of the flag shows the "Southern Cross," a group of stars seen in the southern hemisphere all year. The seven-pointed star in the lower left stands for Australia's six original states and its territories.

Australian money is called the Australian dollar. There are 5, 10, 20, and 50-cent coins and one- and two-dollar coins. There are also 5, 10, 20, 50, and 100-dollar notes. Most Australian coins feature Australian animals and the notes feature famous Australian people. In September 2003, one U.S. dollar equaled 1.5 Australian dollars.

Glossary

continent One of the seven great bodies of land on the earth.
didgeridoo (dee-jer-ree-DOO) A long hollow pipe made from a tree log.
eucalyptus (yoo-kah-LIP-tiss) An evergreen tree that grows in hot regions.
marsupial (mar-SOO-pee-uhl) A kind of animal whose babies are carried in a pouch.
nocturnal Active at night.
plateau (pla-TOE) A broad area of high, flat land.
shear (SHEER) To cut or clip off hair or wool.
snorkel To swim underwater using a short, curved tube in the mouth to breathe.
symbol A mark or sign that stands for something else.
unique Being the only one, having nothing like it.

Fast Facts

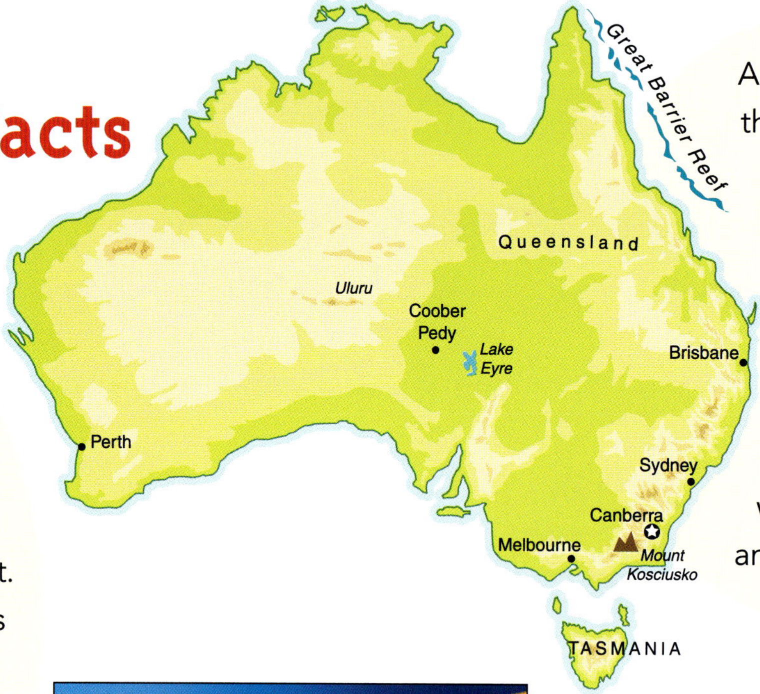

Australia is the smallest of the world's seven continents. It is also the largest island in the world. It is about the size of the United States, without Hawaii and Alaska.

Australia's official name is the Commonwealth of Australia. It has a democratic government. The head of Australia's government is the prime minister. A parliament makes laws for the country.

Australia's climate changes from place to place, but it is generally warm and dry. Much of the land is desert, or semidesert. These areas are called the outback.

In the top left corner of the Australian flag is the Union Jack, the British flag. The right half of the flag shows the "Southern Cross," a group of stars seen in the southern hemisphere all year. The seven-pointed star in the lower left stands for Australia's six original states and its territories.

The capital city, Canberra, is in the east. *Canberra* is an Aboriginal word meaning "meeting place." The Aborigines were Australia's first people.

In Australia, 26.1 percent of the people are Anglican, 26 percent are Roman Catholic, 24.3 percent are other Christian religions, 11 percent are non-Christian, and 12.6 percent are other religions.

English is the official language of Australia.

Australian money is called the Australian dollar. There are 5, 10, 20, and 50-cent coins and one- and two-dollar coins. There are also 5, 10, 20, 50, and 100-dollar notes.

Australia's tallest peak, Mount Kosciusko, is in the Australian Alps. It is 7,316 feet (2,231 m) tall.

Right in the center of Australia is Uluru. It is the largest rock in the world. It is 1.5 miles (2.4 km) long, 1 mile (1.6 km) wide, and about 1,142 feet (348 m) high. Uluru looks like it is glowing a deep red color.

As of July 2004, there were 19,913,144 people living in Australia.

Proud to Be Australian

Evonne Goolagong Cawley (1951–)

Evonne Goolagong Cawley was born in the Riverina District of New South Wales. She is one of Australia's most famous tennis players. Her father was a sheepshearer and her mother raised Evonne and her seven brothers and sisters. Her fondest childhood memories are of visiting the tin shacks of her Aboriginal relatives. She was good at all sports, but loved tennis. At the age of five she joined the tennis club, even though she was too young. In 1971, at age nineteen, she became the first Aboriginal Australian to win Wimbledon. Evonne went on to win the Australian Open four times and the French Open once. She won Wimbledon again in 1980. Altogether, she won ninety-two professional tournaments.

Reverend John Flynn (1880–1951)

Reverend John Flynn was the founder of the Royal Flying Doctor Service. He was nicknamed "Flynn of the Inland." He was born in Victoria, the youngest of three children. He graduated from secondary school in 1898 and became a teacher. He decided to become a minister and studied at Melbourne University. He became interested in working as a missionary in the outback. There, he saw how difficult life was for the people, and how far they lived from medical help. He became the head of the new Australian Inland Mission (AIM). At first, he and other ministers traveled in the outback by camel or horseback. Although traveling by airplane was still brand new, Flynn saw it as a better way to get medical help to people in the outback. He began to raise money for this cause, and in 1928 the Aerial Medical Service was started. In 1933, the church gave the service to the government to run. It became the Australian Aerial Medical Service, the Flying Doctor Service, and then Royal Flying Doctor Service. Reverend Flynn died in 1951 and was buried at Alice Springs, in the heart of the outback. He and the Royal Flying Doctor Service of Australia are on the Australian twenty-dollar bill.

Greg Norman (1955–)

Greg Norman was born in Queensland, Australia, on February 10, 1955. As a teenager, he loved outdoor sports, such as swimming, fishing, and rugby. When he was sixteen, he went along with his mother while she played golf. It sparked an interest that created one of the greatest golfers in history. He became a professional in 1976. He was nicknamed "The Great White Shark" because of his "killer" drive to win. He won the British Open Championship in 1986 and 1993. He won twenty U.S. Professional Golfers Association (PGA) Tour titles. In total, Norman has won eighty-six professional events around the world. He held the number one world ranking for 331 weeks.

Find Out More

Books

The Continents: Australia by April Pulley Sayre. Twenty-First Century Books, Connecticut, 1998.

Enchantment of the World: Australia by Ann Heinrichs. Children's Press, Connecticut, 1998.

Exploring Cultures of the World: Australia, The Land Down Under by Jacqueline Drobis Meisel. Benchmark Books, New York, 1997.

Welcome to My Country: Australia by Peter North and Susan McKay. Gareth Stevens Publishing, Wisconsin, 1999.

Web Sites*

Find maps, facts, and geographical information at
http://www.ga.gov.au/education/facts/

Learn about the Prime Minister's office and Parliament at
www.pm.gov.au/aus_in_focus/kids/

Video

Australia's Great Barrier Reef. VHS, 60 minutes. National Geographic, 1998.

*All Internet sites were available and accurate when sent to press.

Index

Page numbers for illustrations are in **boldface.**

maps, 5, 42

Aborigines, 8, 9, **13**, 13–15, 17, **17**, 25, 42, 44
animals, 10, **11**, 11–13, **12**, 19, **19**
architecture, **14**, **21**, 32, **32**
art, 14, 17

beaches, **28**, 28–29, **29**, 34
birds, 9, **9**, 13
   song about, 27
bridges, **32**

Cawley, Evonne Goolagong, 44, **44**
cities, **4**, **5**, 7, 21, **21**, 31–32, **32**, 36
   capital, 7, **14**, 42
climate, 4, 6–7, 42
clothing, 24, **24**, **25**, 33, **33**, 37
coast, 6, 7, **7**, 28–29
communication, 18–19, 26, **26**
coral, 7–8

dance, 17
danger, 18, 29
desert, 4, 6, **6**
   See also outback

energy, 7
ethnic groups, 13–14, **15**, 15–16

fairs, 38
families, 21, 31–32
farming, 7
   See also sheep and cattle
fences, 19
fireworks, **36**
flag, 40, **40**
Flynn, Reverend John, 44–45
food, 16, 21–23, **22**, 29–30, 34
   recipe, 23
forests, 4–6, 7

games, 25, 31, 33, **33**
gemstones, 19–20, **20**
government, **14**, 15, 42
Great Barrier Reef, **7**, 7–8
greetings, 16, **16**

health care, 18–19, 29, 44–45
history, 13, 36–37
holidays, **34**, 34–39, **35**, **36**, **39**
horses, 31, 38, **38**
housing, 20–21, **21**, 29, 44

immigration, **15**, 15–16
inventions, 14–15

jobs, 19

lakes, 8
language, 14, 16, 43
   unique words, 4–6, 16, 21, 22, 29, 30
leisure, 25, **28**, 28–32, **29**, **31**
location, 4

mining, 19–20, **20**
money, 12, 40, **40**, 43
mountains, 6, 32, 43, **43**
music, 17, **17**, 32
   songs, 27, 35, 39, **39**

name, 15, 42
neighboring countries, 4, **5**
Norman, Greg, 45, **45**

oceans, 4
outback, 4, 18–19, 26, **26**, 31, **31**, 42, 44–45

parades, **37**, 37–38
patriotism, 36–38, **37**
plants, 6, **10**, 10–11, 35
plateau, 6
population data, 6, 13, 43
ports, **4**

products, 19–20, **20**
   See also sheep and cattle
races, 38, **38**
religion, 8, 16, 17, 24, 32, 43
restaurants, 21, 29
rock formations, 8, **8**, 43, **43**
rural areas. *See* outback

school, **24**, 24–26, **25**, **26**
seasons, 4, 34, **34**
sharks, 29
sheep and cattle, 7, 11, 19, 38
shopping, 18, 22, 34, 36
size, 4, 42
skies, 40
social life, 31–32
songs, 27, 35, 39, **39**
sports, 25, 29, **29**, 30, **30**, 33, **33**, 38
   famous athletes, 44, 45
states, 40
surfing, 29, **29**, 34

television, 31
territories, 40
theater, 32
transportation, 12, **18**, 18–19, 25, **25**, 44–45
trees, **10**, 11, 12, 17, 35
   See also forests

universities, 26

vacations, 26
veterans, **37**, 37–38

water, 6–7
Web sites, 46

47

About the Author

Sharon Gordon has written many nature and science books for young children. She has worked as an advertising copywriter and a book club editor. She is writing other books for the *Discovering Cultures* series. Sharon and her husband Bruce have three teenage children, Douglas, Katie, and Laura, and one spoiled pooch, Samantha. They live in Midland Park, New Jersey. The family especially enjoys traveling to the Outer Banks of North Carolina. After she puts her three children through college, Sharon hopes to visit the many exciting places she has come to love through her writing and research.